Love/War

Nordisk Books
www.nordiskbooks.com

First published by Norstedts, Sweden 2016
Translated from Århundradets Kärlekskrig
Copyright © Ebba Witt-Brattström

This translation first published by Nordisk Books 2017
Published by agreement with Norstedts Agency
Translation copyright © Kate Lambert 2017

Published with the financial support of the
Swedish Arts Council

Cover design © Nice to meet you

Printed in Great Britain by Clays Ltd, St Ives plc

A CIP catalogue record for this book is available from the British Library

ISBN 9780995485228

Love/War

Ebba Witt-Brattström

Translated by Kate Lambert

nordisk books

Hommage à Märta Tikkanen & August Strindberg

He said:
If you abandon me
all you can expect
is life-long hate.

She said:
I think either
I or you
must die.

DANCE OF DEATH

He said:
I suppose this morning
wasn't worse
than usual.

It won't get
any better than this.
It's far more probable
that from now on
goodwill
on either side
will decrease
by a few percentage points
a week.

I don't know
what could possibly
turn that process
around.

Why don't you
ask your therapist?

She said:
I did.
He wants me
to give you
an ultimatum:
we go to therapy
you go to therapy
or I leave you.
Don't shoot the messenger.

He said:
I'm not ever going back.
He's a charlatan
like all psychoanalysts.

The peace that appears
during therapy is because
due to the relative calm
each party imagines
that the other has given in
and they are about
to get their own way.

But because neither
has in fact given an inch
it is only a matter of time
before hostilities are resumed.

A war doesn't actually end
until one side is
totally defeated
or dead.

She said:
You're talking power politics
my dear.
When lovers are at war
there are no winners
only losers.

A kiss, a bite
The two should rhyme
for one who truly loves
with all her heart
can easily mistake them.

He said:
The precautionary measures

the therapist wanted to teach me
are things I have long observed
anyway
but I might as well
not have bothered.

I still can't shrink myself
to the right format.

She said:
"Precautionary measures".
What sort of expression is that
in a loving relationship?

Why would I
be making you
shrink yourself
to my little format?

He said:
It's amusing really.
It's like the UN.
The chap in his corner
doesn't know
what sort of people

he's dealing with.
He's a gentleman amateur.

His good advice
doesn't apply to
clients like us
who have been
sharpening our knives
for ages.

Peace be upon him.
Have a nice day.

She said:
Can you hear what you're saying?
That I'm a dwarf
and you're a titan
incapable of lowering yourself
to my level.

In other words
precisely the arrogance
and the contempt for me
and our relationship
that so effectively kills

my feelings for you.
It's all pitch black now.

He said:
The fact that it is all pitch black
is a perfectly correct observation
but I find it neither new
nor particularly perceptive.

I no longer want
your trust.
It is purely arbitrary
in any case
and depends on
your moods.

And it doesn't take much
to piss you off.
In fact
it doesn't take anything at all.

So whatever I do
or say
is totally
irrelevant.

She said:
My therapist says
I have all the symptoms
of an abused woman.

He said:
Calling yourself
an abused woman
is simply boasting.

It would at least be slightly interesting if you were.

But your crushed vanity
isn't interesting in the slightest
because there's so much of it about
these days
especially among women.

She said:
Slow handclap.
You really are an expert
at power games.

You managed to tick off all the tactics –
minimising

generalising
ridiculing
plus one dismissive sneer.

He said:
Can we stop
all this childishness please?

And can we be clear
that I am not
a candidate for therapy?

I will view any further suggestions
in that direction
as acts of hostility
as I will every attempt
to disrupt or explicitly
disparage my activities
in private or in public.

I say explicitly
because I despise
guesswork and
argumentum ex silentio.

She said:

The unhappiness makes my skin crawl.

Normality – this state of humiliation.

Not being able to rely on

the person you are closest to.

In the Gulag

it was the hopelessness

that was worst.

A slow death.

I am a borderline

post-mortem case.

You said I killed you – haunt me then!

He said:

No shrink in the world

could make you human.

She said:
When did our love become
this calculated malice?
It's gone so far that I want you dead.

As if you were vermin
with no right to live
a disease-infested polecat
a puking plague rat
a foul pest.

But who made me this person?

She said:
When did you stop
apologising when you
insulted me
belittled me
sneered at me?

Raged like a lunatic
threw the candlestick
the teapot
the chair at me.

He said:
I see that you are suffering.
But I can't help you
because it is me
that is the problem.

She said:
It was all a misunderstanding was it?
A bad dream.
An operatic trial of love
like The Magic Flute.

How stupid can you get?
Brudertier, Du.

She said:
I'm a prisoner
in your power mechanism.

She said:

Is it possible to live without love?
I no longer desire anything
make no demands of life.
I've learned my lesson.

Gaslight

But why must women be punished?
Mother's fault
it's always mother's fault.

MUM ROWS THE BOAT
DAD IS FUN
as the reading scheme put it

He said:
Mother
how can you trust her?
When once upon a time
she abandoned you to the wolves.

She said:
As a couple we were utterly banal.
You could order us by the dozen.

What a joke.
Thinking ourselves unique.
Après nous le déluge.

How much salt
will be rubbed
into that wound?

He said:
Can't you keep to the point?

She said:
There are situations
in a marriage that
as in works of art
contain condensed meaning
and a symbolic charge.

The pattern only emerges
on rereading.

Was I catfished?

THE GAME IS UP

She said:
Everything I lived for
believed in
wanted
loved
lies burning around me.

Piles of smoking ash
wherever I look.

He said:
Sorry
but I don't want therapy
only to live normally
the way I am
with my vanity
or whatever you want to call it.

If you don't want to
be with me on the ride
any more what can I do?

I am not re-education material
not for my sake
or for anyone else's.

Jedes Leben sei zu führen,
Wenn man sich nicht selbst vermißt;
Alles könne man verlieren,
Wenn man bleibe, was man ist.

She said:
That was a clear answer at least.
You are you and that's that.
The greatest and best
all finished and complete.

The worst Goethe in the business.
Dummkopf.

He said:
That said – let us be honest here –
I have not overcome my original feelings for you.
Far from it.

Those brief moments
when your voice takes on
a slightly gentler note
are utter bliss
though I'm embarrassed by it
when the atmosphere then turns sour.

It isn't easy
making your way
on the road of life.

She said:
Golden lads and girls all must,
as chimney-sweepers, come to dust.
Ta-ra

I AM NOT YOUR LITTLE DOG WOOF WOOF

He said:
What I do with my life
after you
has nothing to do with you.

What are you going to do yourself?
Find yourself a beta male
who you can preach to
without him protesting?

Who won't steal your limelight.
There are probably men like that out there somewhere.
You can ask your feminist cunts.

She said:
Limelight.
Preach.
Feminist cunts.
Who are you?

ALL ROME TREMBLED BEFORE HIM!

He said:
When did you
actually
stop listening?
I need to work it out.

She said:
I never stopped listening
but I can't hear anything
other than your unrelenting
male paranoia.

About me being out to get you
wanting to re-educate you.
What for?

She said:
The Marriage Act
talks about consideration
and consultation.

Yes
the law should be followed

as you're only too eager to insist
when you're the one who benefits.

You are who you are
and always have been
and shall be for ever
amen.

Time for the congregation to burst into hymns of praise.

She said:
But then you haven't
listened to me for years.
Not since I started being miserable.
That didn't suit the lovely image
of the perfect couple did it?
It tarnished it.

He said:
I don't understand a word
you're going on about.
And I don't think
you do either.

He said:

Philanthropy is simply vanity.

Charity is the way

ambitious ladies

keep score.

You with your little

gender equality department.

Who cares.

He said:

When do you ever think

about anything other than

how injured you are

and how appalling it is

that people don't think

you're a great authority.

Why should I play a role in your farce
when you won't play one in mine?
Or do you think yours is less farcical?
How blind can you be?

She said:
I am playing a role in your farce
though it's more of a sordid tragedy.

It's sad that
all you can do is
sneer at me
but that's fine
I'm used to it.
I've done the weekend shop.
Don't destroy it
please.

YOU CAN GET A LOT DONE
BETWEEN THE TEARS

She said:
In *The Night of the Tribades*
Siri cries
I'm so alone.

Enquist gets it spot on there.
But then the play is from 1975.
Women were on the move.
And new men too.

He said:
I hate the seventies.
No-one noticed me.

He said:
It's emancipation.
It put ideas in women's
heads.

Feminism is
a fixed set of opinions.
I despise that kind of thing.

He said:
Man is superior to woman.
It's how it's always been
and how it's going to stay.

Haven't you got any nails
to bite

or chairs
to hit?

She said:
The mechanism in place.
Half the brain switched off.

Your Google translate
takes the things I say.
Prints out
evasive
derisive
dismissive
contemptuous
words.
Nonsense.

Are you a human being or a platitude generator?

He said:
Watch your step.
I can be a really nasty person.

She said:
Think that's news?

Today my sister
saw the bruises
in the bath.

She said:

According to the divorce advice

on the internet

when you stop wanting

to do things together

it's over.

IF WE WERE IN AGREEMENT

He said:

I acknowledge

that I am always

in some sense

dissembling.

Tense.

I am only relaxed

in brief glimpses.

But it's what
my position
demands.

She said:
Constantly finding oneself
in bad company
makes one
a bad person.

He said:
I am proud of myself.
No-one cares about
your whining
anyway.

All that women stuff has had its day.

She said:
You are over-symbolised in my life.
Like I am in yours —
phallic mother.
Yuck.

Was nun kleiner Mann

She said:
My therapist said
"This is an example of a type of man
that has to float above.
He can only think in terms of
superior and inferior.
Dominance or submission.
Only accepts uncritical admiration.

As long as you were part of
his grandiose projects
you were good enough.

He is threatened by your successes.
He can only relate to people as rivals.
Don't take it personally."

He said:
I don't compete with women.

She said:
Parasite.
Was I merely
a host for you
until another

bigger

fatter

host

came along?

CHASTISE ME LIKE A DOG

He said:

It's got nothing to do with you.

He said:

Strindberg became *persona non grata*

for *The New Kingdom*.

Not for his hatred of women.

She said:

You can get that from Wikipedia.

So why do you think

The Father and Miss Julie

were rejected then?

He said:

Oh piss off.

And stop moaning

you fucking cunt.

She said:

Nora's mistake –

believing in miracles.

RELY ON A MAN AND YOU DESERVE SLAPPING

You're a mouldering tree stump in our home.

But better that than

when you explode and

start hitting things.

He said:

You shouldn't get so het up

about people's behaviour.

She said:

You go around with your eyes shut

and your hands over your ears.

All you hear is the buzz

of the arse-lickers' cheering.

He said:

Your intellectual vanity

was greater than your goodness.

Too bad.

You're the thought police.

She said:
You were gathering evidence against me
when I hadn't even been
called to trial.

I have to force myself
to see clearly
despite the knifepoint of betrayal
twisting deeper inside me.

You can beat me to death
but I won't give in –
what you felt wasn't love
never has been.

WILFUL DISREGARD

She said:
Great emotion is
a lonely grave
when it doesn't
find its equal
in the other.

Serfdom
Stockholm syndrome
Bride abduction.

Deus ex machina.
Come and get me
Medea.

She said:
Love is like opera
absurd pretentious rubbish
if you don't give in to it
allow yourself to be moved by it.

He said:
Wagner's Senta is an Elsa
who does her duty
by unselfishly
throwing herself into the sea and dying
to save the Dutchman
from his curse.

She said:
Do you feel excommunicated?
A perverted credo

that I don't hear.
But then nor do you.

Your ideology is so alien to me.
Your power politics intolerable.

Le repos du guerrier

He said:
I make every effort
to provoke you
as little as possible
but sometimes
the retorts
say themselves.

He said:
If I believed you loved me
I'd think I was God.

She said:
Yeah, right.
The Seducer's Diary
Johannes:
"If I were a God

I would do for Cordelia
what Neptune did for a nymph.
I would transform her into a man."
Aren't you ashamed of yourself?

She said:
Picking your way through the ruins
of a life-long relationship
suspecting that
there were never any
shared foundations
in the first place.

Just a launch pad
for an arriviste
dürstend nach Ruhm und Ehre.

He said:
I have only made the choices
a man can make in his life.

She said:
If this was an opera
you would now
tell me

in the last act
that it had all been
a test of my love.

We would fall into each other's arms
and walk hand in hand
into the sunset
singing our final aria
to life.

That's why I need opera.
I can't live with the
disappointment
of reality.

Lasciatemi morire.

She said:

You will always be a puzzle to me.

Why throw away

the only life you have?

On showing off.

He said:

I'm a completely normal narcissist.

She said:

It's all about charm with you.

She said:

You're always thinking

what's in it for me.

The waking prayer

of the psychopath.

The feminist prays:

Dear Lord grant me the courage

again today

to put up with

the insults

the ignoring

the trivialisation

the violence.

BUT OF TERROR WAS THE MAIL-COAT CAST AND
OF SHAME

He said:

Political women

are the scum of the earth.

Wagner knew that.

She said:

And Hitler

and Stalin

and Osama bin Laden.

He said:

You're committing high treason.

You know what the punishment is
for that.

She said:
I tell it like it is.
You can't stand that.

He said:
I will kill you.
Not metaphorically
literally.

She said:
So that's your definition
of an act of war:
me puncturing your
pompous life-long lie.

I knew it.
It was all fake.
Dopey.

He said:
A man must decide in his own house.

She said:
Feels good, does it?
The air cleared
the cupboard in the right place
the old bat in her corner.

Wow
at last you get to
flex your muscles.
Hate and punish.
Hear the Titans roar.

I'll pray to the
holy Madonna
for you.

He said:
Listen
you puffed up little cunt.
Why don't you try doing something good some time.

She said:
These days I think
with the crusts cut off
like toast.

He said:

I've always wanted to be

il capo di capo.

She said:

Who do you think you are?

Napoleon?

He said:

A man always marches with his troops.

Dedicates himself totally to the mission

Gives the group his complete and full approval.

Wondering about your feelings

is third or fourth on the list.

She said:

It didn't work very well

on the Eastern Front.

He said:

This is how it is.

I don't know what

might be going on

in my dark depths.

Whose fault is that?
Mine of course
if one accepts the hypothesis
that I am wrong
was wrong from the start
have always been
and always will be wrong.
And because I am wrong
I have no case to bring before you.

So I'm sat there again
humming the same eternal song:
I am wrong.

You'll be humming it to the day you die.

She said:
It's not you that's wrong
silly.
It's your actions towards me
that are wrong.

You say you would rather
be a public figure
than a private person

because in the public sphere you are right.
In the private sphere you are wrong
because that's what I –
your tormentor – think.
As if it was a law of nature.

Have you forgotten?
When others thought you were wrong
I thought you were right.
I was good enough then.

Then you abandoned me.
It only took a second.
Power called.
So I became wrong.
Because otherwise you
couldn't have been
right.

God preserve us from
people who are right.

He said:
I wish I could be you.
And if I couldn't be you

I wish I could be like you.
Serious.
It would make everything
so much simpler
or at least possible.

But I'm not like you.
I'm different.
In other words wrong
I feel I immediately have to add that
to match
the tone
of our conversation.

But I am so tired of
feeling wrong.
No-one should have to
go around feeling
that they are wrong.

She said:
Why aren't I falling apart?

He said:
You didn't treat me

like that at the beginning.
You thought I could be improved
but you didn't think
I was wrong.
You wanted to inspire me
to be better.
Not force me.
I liked that.

But somewhere along the way
first you lost patience
then your sense of humour
and finally faith.

But why?
Why shouldn't I
be allowed to be
who I am?

She said:
I'm the biggest dumping ground for misery
in Northern Europe.

Can't you stop talking
about yourself?

He said:

But

you will then respond

with a certain amount of justification:

Do I

your wife

get to be

who I really am?

Aren't my nature

my needs

constantly denied

in our life together?

Don't I have to feel

every time

we are confronted by your world

that I am wrong

have the wrong opinions

champion them the wrong way

react the wrong way?

Can't you see how

deadly this is?

That's how it would go.

Granted.

True enough.

So I suppose that you and I

have the same fundamental experience

although we articulate it differently.

Our life is a double disaster.

It has led to

both you and I

albeit for different reasons

going around as if damned

feeling that what we do and say is wrong

that we are wrong.

He said:

But that's horrendous.

Suppose that you felt you were right.

That you only encountered people

for whom you were right

that you were only in contexts

in which you were right.

Put simply:

that you were living as if in my world

where everything was determined
by your own choices.

Would you then think
that I was wrong
or care so much
about what happened to
be wrong with me?

I don't think so.
You would with gentle
and perhaps amused indulgence
leave me to be who I am
while waiting for me to
see the light.

For me too the problem
would thus be solved
because there is no longer
anyone in my world
who thinks I am radically wrong
other than you.

So.
So perhaps we must

in the end
live separate lives –
You according to your head
Me according to mine.

She said:
Who are you trying to convince?
I've been trying
to tell you exactly that
for ten years.
Let me go.

HUGO RASK WAS NOT UNDER ANY OBLIGATION TO LOVE HER

He said:
The basic problem seems to be
if this daft little analysis
holds water
that I tried to
organise you into a life that
doesn't suit you at all
and that you reacted
by trying to change this life
by trying to change me

which proved to be
far too difficult a task.

She said:
This never-ending
mansplaining.

If you'd listened to me
instead of
bullying
reprimanding
correcting
oppressing
threatening
tormenting me
we would be free now.

Maybe friends.
Maybe lovers again.

He said:
You talk such crap.
No-one tells me
what to do.

THE SUN NEVER RISES

He said:
It was glorious.
Terrible to be so enslaved.

She said:
What sort of response is that
to making love.

He said:
I had a dream.
I was fucking you
but you were only fucking me
to save your husband.
I enjoyed it very much.

She said:
Am I just

an alibi for your fantasies.
Wank fodder.

Mimetic desire

He said:
I knew telling you was a stupid idea.

She said:
If people only knew
what an unerotic dick you are.

It's hardly any wonder
you're so insensitive about
how a woman works.
I'd have thought you'd have
got the hang of it
unterwegs.

He said:
My sexuality is
simple and raw but robust.
I have no intention
of apologising for it.

Whatever you
and your semi-tribades say.
When did you get tired
of the erotic game?

She said:
When I realised
that for you
it wasn't a game
it was serious.

She said:
What is infidelity
if not that –
never opening up
to your partner.

You've got your revolting internet porn.
What have I got?
My pathetic dream
of intimacy.

WHAT'S IN A NAME IT IS NOR HAND
NOR FOOT NOR ANY OTHER PART OF MAN

He said:
With you in Vienna
I thought I'd found
a way out
an escape from the pride and prestige.

She said:
Vienna was
the quenching of the last hope.
The terror like acid in my body
when I approached our home
a torture chamber.

He said:
Vienna was a rebirth.
But now I'm once more
drugged by
the sweetness of praise.

She said:

What are you going to do with the

black ravens

of anxiety

in your chest

when it all stops?

COLD HEART BENEATH THE GLITTER

GREY SKIN, BRIGHT RIBBON CURLED

He said:

Where did you think I would end up?

Beneath you?

She said:

You only get

one version of life.

What good will your position

do you

if no-one cries at your funeral?

He said:

Only children think

reality is real.

She said:
Life is about
maturing beyond
the age of five.

He said:
Idealisation demands loss.
The real object must not mar the ideal.
You are too close.

ORPHEUS AND EURYDICE

He said:
The present is just a seam
between the past
and the future.

The most important thing
is the magical effect
of the grand moment
that reverberates down the years –
my exaltation.

You have no concept of that.

She said:

When the gods hit back

they hit hard.

You're suffering from hubris.

Remember Agamemnon's red carpet.

Clytemnestra's revenge.

She said:

I went to the therapist

to hear:

"I hear what you're saying."

I go to church

to hear:

"The Lord make his face to shine upon you."

When will your face shine upon me?

Aus den Augen aus dem Sinn

Suspicion is all that is

holding us together.

He said:

What are men ultimately looking for in women?

Beauty?

Only to begin with.

Sex?

For a while before that palls.

Comradeship?

Hardly.

A touch of excitement in our existence?

There's enough of that already.

No

we're looking for goodness.

Motherliness?

I say goodness.

A real mother is good – naturally

but that doesn't mean

that the man is looking for a new mother

in his beloved.

He is looking for goodness:

the only thing man

cannot live without.

She said:

Alice on Edgar:

"He's the sort of man who says what he thinks and then

believes it."

He said:

I built my life

on the assumption

that your goodness was greater

than your professional vanity.

That proved to be incorrect.

You are furious

that I don't take you seriously

as a professional woman

as a feminist.

But I find it difficult

to relate to what you do

in your Department

and that means I don't know

what value I am to place on it.

She said:

You have to be able to do that

in an equal couple.

He said:

We are not an equal couple.

I don't compete with girls.

Like all women

you are hypocrisy
all the way through.

You're suffering from crushed self-esteem.
That's all there is to it.
It isn't any more complicated than that.
There's no cure for it.

She said:
Was it you who set up
hurt.white.man.org?

He said:
In a war, the most important tactic is perseverance.
You have to give your opponent time
to make serious mistakes.

She said:
Is that why you were never
upfront with me?
What a serious mistake.

My lack of trust
is merely a reflection of yours
once I finally twigged.

He said:

I don't consider myself to be perfect

but a man doesn't need

to be perfect.

She said:

People talk about unhappy love.

Huh.

That's nothing.

The really terrible thing is

the icy loneliness

of half-dead love.

By the time it finally dies

you are already dead.

He said:

You dropped me.

I hate you.

Go away.

You shit on everything around you.

And don't start crying again

pig cunt.

He said:
I couldn't entertain the thought
that a woman
who had declared her love for a man
who was captivated by him
could be capable
of killing him.

Now I know better.

She said:
I am
Penthesilea
Cassandra
Sappho.
Not Pallas Athena
leaping from the head
of the father-god.

He said:

OK.

When I shut you out

I lost.

The adventure ended when the demons

of self-importance seized power.

You became the wife

my work a jerry-built

monument.

Nothing was fun after that.

She said:

I am here

nothing is too late.

See me.

I am your beloved.

HURRY MY DEAREST COME HURRY TO LOVE ME
MINUTE BY MINUTE THE DAYS THEY GROW DARK

He said:
The Board is
the first refuge of the egotist.

Relinquishing egotism
is exactly like saying no to
a personality-changing drug.

It hurts at the time but
once the decision is made
it is nothing but endless relief.

Without the illusion of greatness
the guaranteed pension
the benefits that distinguish me
from the populace
the activities themselves are trivial
and relatively insignificant.

The role played by luck
that is instantly forgotten
when appointing members to the Board.

She said:

I'll make you alive again.

Come in I'll give you shelter from the storm.

He said:

Love is the foremost delight

that consoles us for our existence.

Without that to spice it up

life is dull and sleepy

tedium triumphs.

She said:

Love is not a delight

on top of everything else.

Love is life

our daily bread.

He said:

Divorce is like

an earthquake.

If you're lucky you get to watch

your world collapse.

If you're unlucky

you fall headlong

down into the depths
never to be rescued.

She said:
Stop feeling sorry for yourself
I'm still here and
I'm suffering too.

She said:
Talk to me.

He said:
My death would solve
all my family's problems
and lots of other people's too.

It would release you
from my company
and allow you to mourn
our lost love.

It would provide money
for our offspring
that they could use
to set themselves up in life.

It would leave a place free
on the Board to be grabbed
by some overjoyed careerist.

Often the best thing a person
can do is die
and make room for others.
It's an overcrowded arena
rife with impatience.

No-one apart from you
would be sad
not really.
Strange how life dissipates
a person's motivation
for existing.

She said:
Blah blah.
Blah blah.
Blah blah.

He said:
Dying young
would have been preferable.

Everyone who knew
would have stood round the coffin.

She said:
We are still here.
Your people.
A threadbare little group
who once knew who you were.

He said:
Do you remember the pond where we
hired little boats and sailed with the children?
It must be twenty years ago now.

You sat on a bench in the sun.
No suspicions
a genuine union.
Today it's incomprehensible.

We couldn't even imagine
that objective antagonism
could arise between us.

The children came first of course.

And then all the abominations.
Incomprehensible

tragic
a dreadful fate.

He said:
Our family is falling apart
And I who never thought
any accidents could happen
on that front.

What could defeat our love?

Now I know.
There is no way back.

She said:
You always start from the wrong end.
The children are the fruit
of our love which
is
was
number one.

You talk about fate but you mean
your comfort.

He said:
Your unbelievable
flawless smugness
giving the victim the upper hand.

He said:
I look at you
and I ask myself
if a woman's vanity is increased
by living with a successful man.

She said:
That was the stupidest thing
I've ever heard.
Even from you.

He said:
The women learned
and copied but slowly
and hesitantly.

It's only in our own time
that all the barriers
seem to have come down.

What literary arts
have made the greatest strides
in the past twenty years?

Chicklit and cookbooks.

She said:
No
it's more like
male self-pity
has flooded the market.

He said:
It's female to
reclaim the stories.
You remember everything.
I immediately forget
what doesn't interest me.

She said:
Love isn't a balloon
you can hug when you need it.
Do and it shrivels.

He said:
The claims power makes to exclusivity.
If you're not in the club
you don't know what the score is.
That's always given rise to aggression.

Isn't that what's sabotaging our marriage
rather than different values?

Both of us should be equally
uninterested in this fantasy world
or
like-mindedly
love its representation
the beautiful art of hypocrisy.

Generally this is hard to achieve.
Disinterest is always an option of course.
It allows you to unite in contempt
of the elite.

She said:
I have never demanded more of you
than to not let yourself be
consumed

quenched by the psychosis of conceit

not overdose on

the drug of vanity

every hour

day

week

month

year

of the only life we have.

So there is still

a little bit

of the man I loved

left.

He said:

Our matrimonial debacle –

The marriage of Pride and Envy

bred fury.

She said:

I don't know about envy.

I want to be a decent human being.

Your megalomania

terrifies me.

I feel sadness
and fury that
you tricked me
abandoned me.

You loved
on false pretences.
Disappointment is the air I breathe.

He said:
Well you must have been
a little fool
to fall for me then.

I have only done
what every man
has the right to do
in his life.

You have no part in my decisions.

He said:
If you can't behave
you had better leave.

She said:
And you get to decide that?

BITE MY TONGUE

He said:
I decide that
yes.

He said:
You're mentally ill.
That's what the problem is.

He said:
Everyone is corrupt
they can all be bought.

They are
egotists
mean
average
cretins.

She said:
You only think that

because your network
consists of
creeps and sycophants.

He said:
I love servility.

He said:
Loneliness is
an indescribable state.
The loss of life
becomes assets
capital in the bank.

Credit is a transfer.
Appreciation generated by means of infection.

ADVERTISE OR GO UNDER

She said:
Was that my greatest crime?
Failing to admire
your self-deception.
Only loving you outside your role.
So uninteresting.

He said:

Those who achieve success

become cynical.

Those who don't

become bitter.

She said:

Plague or cholera.

Me or you.

Life or death.

He said:

I have forgiven all my enemies

I never think about them.

They don't interest me.

They weren't talented enough

otherwise they

would have crushed me.

But you preferred to claim

the moral high ground

Unfairly treated.

An unrewarding role

as you might have noticed.

He said:

No-one dares to say

that I am reactionary.

Just you

and no-one

listens to you

anyway.

She said:

Chapter 1, section 2 of the Marriage Act stipulates

that spouses are to show each other

fidelity and consideration.

They are to jointly

care for home and children

and work together in consultation

for the best of the family.

Can you even spell consideration?

Can you even spell consultation?

Can you even spell marriage?

Can you even spell for the best of the family?

He said:

That was rather unnecessary.

He said:

I have no idea what it is you want.

To have the right

to be the one who has the power

put out my lanterns

so that yours can

shine brighter.

Get revenge.

Every time things get

the tiniest bit better between us

you end up finding something else

I have done

said or apparently thought wrong

and then your cheeks start glowing

with rage again.

She said:
Our happiness lay
in the children running in the streets.
In our green aquarium.

When you played for me
while I stood in the dark kitchen.
Always dark kitchens.

Eager voices from upstairs
where the children sat
bent over Lego.

The tenderness between us
our discussions
playful arguments
quarrels
intoxicating reconciliation.

Now I find that you have
piled your defeats up
into a heap.
Nothing forgotten
nothing understood
nothing forgiven.

You're lighting the touch paper.

I am wading through fog
switching between despair
and dissociation.

GIVE ME A GRAVE IN THE LAND OF MY BIRTH

He said:
You are not a proper woman.
A woman should be warm
and devoted to the man.

Your thought processes
your brain
your inquisitorial analytical capacity
scare me.

There has to be
a fairytale element to emotion
or it becomes calculation.

She said:
Speak for yourself.
Your idealisation of
the woman's feelings for the man
doesn't seem to apply to the man's
feelings for the woman.

Love is a story of a couple.
Not the conditional submission
of one party
to the needs of the other.

BE WHITE MAN'S SLAVE

You are only enthralled
by the woman's sacrifice.
You call that love.
My arse.

She said:
Now I have dreamt two nights in a row

that I was happy and carried a knife in my hand,
a bloody knife, and my heart was as light as a bird.

Dreams mean nothing but I wonder
if I shall see the same dream one more time.

He said:
You put that very well.

She said:
Edith Södergran.
And you call yourself educated.

She said:
Alone I came, alone I must go.
My free heart has no brother.

He said:
You are pathetic.

He said:
You are the Dovre witch.

She said:
You are a psychoanalytical nuclear meltdown.

You're constantly giving yourself away
and it infuriates me
because I notice words.

He said:
You just want me to adopt
your opinions.

She said:
I am talking about the defeat of my life.
The shame of realising
in front of the whole world
that this is my husband.
This puffed up
artificial
bully.

Besserwisser.

Well-read
lecturer
master
The sensible one.

She said:

Where did your emotional intelligence go?

Were you faking that too?

When did you lose any sense of shame?

He said:

You make me pay for

all the disappointments

you suffer.

You talk about women

but you're lying to yourself.

It's all about

your lack of success.

Your drive to improve the world is ridiculous.

You have failed.

You weren't good enough.

You're suffering from career envy.

Don't put that on me.

She said:

Negging.

If you are determined to
drive our marriage over a cliff
there is nothing in heaven
or earth
that can stop you.

She said:
You didn't want to be
the brother of my free heart.
That's that then.

AND THEY ALL LIVED UNHAPPILY EVER AFTER

He said:

There's no such thing as female oppression.

Thirty million girls aborted

or killed at birth in China

is merely a matter of custom and stupidity.

Nor is it true

that there are any

unexplained pay differences

between the sexes in Sweden.

It's because men know

how to command a high salary.

She said:

Oh living in this fog

of deranged masculine

smugness.

Every sperm is sacred

She said:
You say that my work
at the Department
is fine because
it stimulates me.

You forget that
it supported all of us
when taking a full-time job
was beneath you.

She said:
In many respects
pride is like
diseases that
destroy people's personalities.
An Alzheimer's of honour.

It eats up the people it has
in its grip.

In the end
all that's left are

some characteristic gestures
facial mimicry
the body's scent.

The soul is gone
the distinctiveness
the spark of life
the openness
the look in their eyes.
Everything that goes to make
them human.

You are your diagnosis.

He said:
You talk so much rubbish.
You all want
me to make myself
a head shorter
to be easier
to deal with.

But I refuse
to consent
to the surgery.

She said:
Death by natural causes.

He said:
You are a half sex.
Your forwardness is male.
You have too many sex hormones
and are therefore predestined
to misery.

She said:
You are a terminator
programmed to
spread fear and
destruction in our lives.

He said:
Real women
know how to manage
the man's natural striving
for dominance.

Learn from the ladies in my world.
If they're cunning
women can gain major advantages.

OH WOMEN OF THE PAST

He said:
The only thing a wife
has the right to demand
is that her husband comes home
and is not unfaithful.

He said:
I won't allow myself
to be scolded by you.
You are out to castrate me.

In everything you do
you're kicking men
in the balls.

She said:
It's the mote and the beam.
It's David and Goliath.

He said:
You're a petty little sister.
You're committing mutiny across the entire fleet.
You just want me to be a copy of you.

I'm not playing a part in your drama.

He said:
Women are always false.
Lying is in your nature.

She said:
So you're a woman then
seeing as you lie so well.

He said:
You're too stupid.
You're more stupid than anyone
has the right to be.
You're governed by envy
the lowest and most treacherous
of all the emotions.

He said:
I never have just one point of view.
I am thinking all the time
changing my opinion
several times a day.
You have to accept that.

She said:
Fine.
Just keep me posted.

She said:
Irretrievable breakdown.
When was official language
so close to the truth.

He said:
You're not in any position
to issue ultimatums.
Don't big yourself up.

She said:
Was our love merely props
from my own
chamber of illusions?

SOMETHING IN THE WAY SHE MOVES

He said:
Everything can be twisted and turned
but I can't forgive you
for stopping fancying me
when I haven't stopped
fancying you.

It's an injustice
much greater than
all the purported disadvantages
that women say they suffer
in our society.

Therefore
your ideology leaves me cold
and your complaints

strike me as trifling
compared with the fact
that you no longer
want to sleep with me.

She said:
I don't fancy you
when you demand that I say:
"Give me your cock, Monsieur".

What porn film did you get that from?
It makes me snigger.

He said:
When someone you're caressing
lies there cold and immobile
like an icicle
it's not something you forget
or are prepared to excuse
whatever else may be
going on.

No arguments
none of your eternal

babbling
justify that
in my eyes.

Of course it isn't a crime
not at all.
Everyone has the right to their feelings
even the negative ones.

But it inspires hate
unless one chooses
to devalue oneself
and I see
no reason
to do that.

She said:
You see no reason to do that.

He said:
Pretend chilliness
I could have accepted.
It's an old female trick
that we men see through.

But this is something different.
Rock solid rejection.

She said:
Could you at least
not run around
naked in the flat
with your flabby
tummy hanging out.

She said:

You talk about a union between us.

But its purpose is to
legitimise the
branding concept of
elite middle-aged man
and feminist hostage.

In the best case I was your sounding board.
A first-class service facility.

I bear an immense burden of guilt.
How many sisters have I tricked?

SHE HAD BEEN ALLOWED TO BE NEAR HIM AS
LONG AS SHE DID NOT SEE HIM FOR WHAT HE WAS

He said:

I have never been contemptuous of what you do yourself.

Never.

It's your monstrous regiment and its spirit

that disturbs me

although I made efforts

not to be provoked

and almost always

faked a smile.

What I feel about the feminist aspect

is roughly what you feel

about my activities on the Board

if your imagination can stretch that far.

She said:

Well yes but my monstrous regiment

has not distorted our life.

As I've said before

I have never lied to you.

Maliciously faked smiles.

It's a lame comparison.

LAME DUCKS

He said:
You are making a serious mistake.
But you don't listen to my answers
so what's the point of taking
this fake dialogue any further.
You have decided how everything is
and don't want your calculations upset.

It isn't the voice of conviction.
It's something else.

You have to shore yourself up
with your moral superiority
be the injured and disappointed party
so that there's absolutely no risk
of the discussion going in any direction
other than the one you have staked out.

It shouldn't be called a conversation.
It's pitiful.

Bloody cunt.

She said:
Hate to be the disappointed party

but it's not as if you gave me much choice.
Decided for me.

You pretended to regret that
in couples therapy
but that was a lie too.
What a depressing slug you are.

He said:
You distort everything I say.
I am trying to tell you
that I would like ten minutes
without your moral superiority
and you answer by calling me
a depressing slug.

Who would have believed you
were capable of that kind of abuse.
Not me at least.
Not even after
all our bloody fights.
You live and learn.

She said:
Note that you are

the man who just called me
a "bloody cunt".

She said:
I lug the shopping bags
up the stairs.
You come down whistling
straight out of the shower in
a nice suit
stinking of aftershave.

Stare at me with cold eyes
as if you'd never seen me before.
Are you pre-senile?

She said:
Why is Professor von X so angry
Virginia Woolf asks
rhetorically.
I know.
It's because women dare to squeak.

Even when I'm lying
knocked down on the kitchen floor
I'm irritating.

"Stop snivelling you puffed up little cunt."

There are
more tears
left
in the sea.

He said:
I don't like the way
you are so collectivist.

Me I am just myself.
Don't swim in the sea any more.

She said:
No
you swim in your goldfish bowl.
Your type of herd animal
is so alien to me.

Thinking is a sport
only for the unafraid
says Undset.
But you
you are afraid.

He said:
Possibly.
If you want a fighter or a warrior
you'll have to
look elsewhere.

She said:
This morning you threw
a teacup at me
lifted the fruit bowl and took aim
locked my wrists
pressed me up against the wall
pursued me raging round the bed
threw me down
forced yourself on me
tried to strangle me.

Who is making that
peculiar screaming noise
I found myself thinking
before help came.

She said:
You really have to do something about
your sudden outbursts of anger

at least try pills.
The violence is escalating
how will this end.

He said:
It's usually only you that drives me mad.
You have only yourself to blame.

She said:
Dr Jekyll and Mr Hyde.
It's not sexy.

He said:
You have failed.
Don't put that on my shoulders.

And I who loved you so much
despite your shortcomings.

She said:
It's more than thirty years ago
we met at that party
and went back to mine.

Today you say
I'm an important part
of your surroundings.
Maybe that's all
I ever was.

Maybe I was just
a safe embrace
primal womb
provider
primary tenant.

NOW IT IS FOR FUCK'S SAKE OVER

He said:
You have never shown
that you needed me.
It's odd
but there it is.

You've always had
a sign up:
I cope on my own.

You never wanted
to show you're weak
but maintained
that Martinsonesque cockiness:
a woman shifts for herself
rely on a man…
etc.

However strong and admirable
it might look
a man does not find
that kind of attitude
welcoming.
It just leaves him standing on the doorstep
swamped with care.

He said:
It cannot be a question
of a true union
because it's about
being free
to ask him to leave
at any time.

I say this with sorrow in my heart
not to reproach you for it.

She said:
I get it.
But it's sad
that you are avenging yourself on my strength
all my hard work for you and the family.

That you have misunderstood everything.
Like the fact that love must be given freely
if it is to last.

L'amour est enfant de bohème

And that the power lovers hold
is not to be used.

When you saw my power die
you despised me even more.
All the times I entreated you
without bitterness
made you enraged.

That was when there was a chance
of true intimacy.

STRONG PEOPLE DON'T BEND
THEY BREAK AND SNAP

She said:
I don't really think you can complain
about my staying power.

Three decades isn't exactly
a brisk "it's not working for me bye."

It frightens me
that you blame
your disappointed love
on me.
Me who loved you to madness.

He said:
You have eloquently explained
that I am surplus to requirements.
What am I supposed to think?

She said:
No
not surplus.
Intolerably
egocentric.

He said:
I only wish to point out
that it is you who doesn't want me.
I am unable to draw
any other conclusion.

She said:
What I don't want is
the Prince of Smugness.

He said:
The same way I don't want
the Saint.

We agree on one point
at least.

She said:
We agree on everything
apart from giving up
this soap opera.
I'm suffocating with anger.

He said:
I'm suffocating with sadness
and dying of high blood pressure
but I have two official functions
to get through today
so I haven't got time
for confrontations.

She said:
Get the message.
You have forfeited
my persistent love.
Schluss.

Living with you is hell:
shit
petty
fake.

There's always a hidden agenda
of contempt for women
underneath the superficial charm.

I forgot:
Cowardly.
Rotten.
And mean
miserly.
Ungenerous.
When did you ever say anything appreciative?

He said:
What was all that about?

Where did that come from?
Even you must realise
that no-one's going to listen
to someone who's yelling like that.

Any mental defective
can spew out
a load of adjectives
but you can't call that
a conversation.

Scenes don't work
and those around us
have every right to avoid them.

You aren't the only person in the world.

She said:
The sack is full.
If you were
the last person on earth
I wouldn't want to touch you.
I hate you.

You're hopeless.
Leave me in peace now please.
I have to work.

He said:
Women always get to
play the innocent.
Because you are
always so terribly oppressed
that everything you do
is excused in advance.

She said:
Is my longing for a man
who loves or at least likes me
an utterly hopeless dream.
Must I abandon it?

SET ME AS A SEAL UPON YOUR HEART

She said:
I feel very sad.
You?

He said:
Yes
it feels hopeless
that we fell back into the mire
again.

She said:
It's a reaction
but it's a flight response.
Completely understandable
but it's better to
embrace the pain.

This is our life now.

He said:
I still prefer
our sunny intervals
of mutual understanding.
There's no sense in suffering.

She said:
Are intervals enough for you?
How self-deluded.

He said:
They're all I've got.
The only times
we talk sensibly to each other.

That's where we have to start
not in the hellish
state of war.

He said:
You want to keep the upper hand
emotionally.
When that doesn't work
you get angry and the whole
hate discourse gushes out.

Personally I don't dare
approach you then
because there is
a 95 percent chance
that I will be kicked in the balls
metaphorically speaking.
And that's the way it goes.

She said:
It's the same for me.
I no longer risk
begging for your attention.

Your viper-like friendliness
is unpredictable in any case.
I never know what's coming next.

Shame yes and ignominy
are the only certainties I've got.

He said:
But isn't it funny how
you always have to have
so many more words than me?

She said:
The one with the power
can maintain a malevolent silence.

He said:
Oh you're so amusing.

DIDI AND GOGO

She said:
I'm not jealous of
your monotonous
stupefying existence.

Coloured spotlights wherever you go.
Seven-star brandy.
Black limousines.

But please examine
your brutality
because it scares me.

He said:
However much sorrow
I may feel
you always have to demonstrate
that you feel more.

We always have to compete
even in the meaningless sport
of being the most innocent
and the most deeply wounded.

OK
I could give up
and declare you the winner
but would that satisfy you?

No
you would want to be right
about everything else as well
ad infinitum:
how we bring up our children
where we live
our sex life
wallpaper
choice of friends
type of pedicure.

If I'm lucky
you might let me
choose the wine.

She said:
You are angry because I stood up for myself.
I haven't been able to influence anything in your life
quite the reverse.

You decided
how we brought up our children
where we lived
our sex life
wallpaper

choice of friends
type of pedicure.

He said:
Look at me.
I have aged ten years
since the war seriously started.
Mocking the man I am today
isn't a fair contest.

You are only satisfied
when you get me to lose my head
because then you can triumphantly
point at my wickedness and say:
See I was right about you.

She said:
You are only honest when you are angry.
That isn't my fault.

The gender war is a shabby power game.

He said:
But in a relationship thirty years old
every failure is shared.

The day we take that
as our starting point
we might get somewhere.

She said:
The Nazis would have loved you.
Obersturmbannführer.

With arrogant authority
you'd have claimed
that the Jews were complicit in
maybe even guilty of
the war waged against them.

Übermensch demands untermensch.

You and your sort
don't want to admit
any guilt
take the slightest responsibility.

How I hate your world.

She said:
How do you know how I would react

if you asked me to forgive you
for mistaking a power battle for love.
What have you got to lose?

She said:
We have lost so many years
in which we could have been happy.
It will always be
a large part of our history.

So I insist:
was your betrayal worth the price
of losing me
and the togetherness
we once had?

Was I worth so little to you?

Do you really think
the only thing a wife can demand
is a spouse who comes home
and isn't unfaithful?

And otherwise he can
roll over his wife and family

like a Soviet tank
pursuing his own agenda.

She said:
You declared war.
Not me.
Everything I said was turned against me.
The regime grew stricter
with every day that passed.

I would be forced to kiss
the hand that hit me
to be able to live in proximity
to your mightiness.
You were the king
I was the beggar maid.

THE TAMING OF THE SHREW

She said:
Try to ask yourself
what you can imagine
sacrificing to live
properly with me
and you will see

what I mean.
It isn't reasonable
for me to bear the guilt
for your life choices.

I'd have managed if you'd have shared.

But your wielding of power
was all about crushing me
enjoying my depression.
It made you feel big.

Our pact goes out of the window
when the Board comes calling.

How can you think
that anyone other than you
can put up with such a dishonest life?

I want to be dealing with simple sensible people
not this smarmy herd of idiots.

She said:
You have won.
I admit that I am

beaten
crushed
broken as a person.

Sorry it shows.

He said:
Finished?
But it isn't all harsh words.
I also clearly see
a bruised
disappointed tenderness.
That's the worst of all.
It just makes me cry.
I go into my office
filled with pictures of you
and feel a dreadful
sadness.

While in many respects
I behaved like an idiot
I think you have
fundamentally
misunderstood me.

Think of the devastation
we will leave behind us
if nothing can halt
the train-wreck.

She said:
Kierkegaard says
life can only be understood backwards
but has to be lived forwards.

Do you truly want to try?

He said:
Though my knees are shaking I am ready.
I have somehow horribly
started to wake from a paralysis
in which my life and yours
were unreal
solely existing
as a tattered backdrop to
my prestige.

It has to do with a kind of duality
that I can only perceive in brief glimpses
like when behind a star

there is another star
visible only as a red gleam
when you gaze
in its direction.

She said:
I am the red star of hope.
Set me aflame.

He said:
I don't understand
how I could
really
have behaved the way I did
unless I assume it's
this double nature
of which I was completely unaware.

If I think about it
I can understand
most of what you have said
and stop feeling hurt
by the rather harsh judgments
that emerged.

I hope
this dawning clarity
doesn't vanish
eclipsed by Mr Hyde.

She said:
Dearest
you can barely guess at
the strength of the love
surging in me.

Don't be afraid.

WHEN YOU WALK THROUGH A STORM

She said:
Will you be able to
accept my love
after all we have been through?
Can we start a genuine life
together?

He said:
Yes
I think I am ready now

on the brink.
Isn't it terrible how bad it had to get.

But the inner resistor is
horrifying.
I call him
the demon of
self-importance.

Now I am starting to see
how he tricked me
and how he distorted
my image of you.

She said:
I don't think
I have ever been
as happy
as you are making me now.

I love you so painfully
with all my bruised heart.
Don't want to lose a second
of your closeness.

I want to listen to you talking to me about us.

He said:
The world we live in
is beset by a dreadful
emotional climate.
We mustn't give in to it.

Once we said to each other
that our love
would astound the world.
Do you remember?

She said:

When you said you don't give a shit about me

I slept well for the first time

in ages.

I'm so desperate

for you to tell me the truth

that I'll take what I can get.

Your hypocrisy

ingratiating grin

turns my stomach.

THE MOOR HAS DONE HIS WORK

THE MOOR MAY GO

She said:

Absurd that in my desperation

I used to think:
I'll divorce him
but he'll hold my hand
when I'm dying.

Now I can't think of
anything worse than
you fouling
my deathbed as well.

She said:
When I see you in the street
I don't even want to say hello.

You look ill
rigid walk
grey mask of a face
jaw muscles stiff.

When weren't you
a psychosomatic wreck?

He said:
I'm sorry to see you
stuck again

in a hallucinatory image of reality.
That was the worst drivel
you've come up with in a very long time.
A bit sad considering that
for a while there
it seemed as though we were on
better terms.
I can't prevent you
from retreating into coldness
like you did the past week
for God knows what reason
and if God does know
he needn't inform me
because it makes no odds.

She said:
You should know that to me
you are the man
who runs from his family
when the avalanche comes.

He said:
Improvements in the relationship
between you and me
are usually illusory

because in the end
you prefer to fall back on
how hurt you are
your only safe harbour.
I hope you like it there.
Bye.

She said:
Each of us is the architect of our own fortune
and I have failed
where you have succeeded.
Simple philosophy.

Divide and rule.
Annex.
Anschluss.

Idiot.
And you want to fuck.
Ha ha.

She said:
Perhaps it is disappointment
not sorrow that terrorises
me.

War alles umsonst

He said:
You stab me in the eye.
Pierce me with needles.
If you hadn't done that
I wouldn't have had to
ignore you.

He said:
You're mad.
It's sad to see someone
become so mad.

She said:
But why am I going mad?
Your soul is black as mud.

He said:
You go around in your own drama
don't properly take part in my life.

She said:
That's because I don't like
the walk-on role

you have assigned to me.

He said:
The woman's job is to be
the sun and the warmth in the man's life.
The sudden change in the weather
in my marriage is a puzzle to me.

Where did the sun go?

She said:
The eclipse was caused
by atmospheric toxicity.

And I'm not your fucking sunshine.
I'm the most important person
in your life:
your one and only woman
and the mother of your children.

A MAN MUST CARRY THE MOTHER OF HIS
CHILDREN IN HIS HANDS

She said:
Don't you get that once upon a time

I fell in love with you
because I mistook you for being the
disobedient son of the patriarchy.

A brave independent thinker
like me.

When you were actually
aiming your bow higher than others'
in order to shoot them down.

How's that for completely taken in.

My defence is
that no-one could
to think so low
of someone they loved.

At least I couldn't.

He said:
I need the halo.
Men fossilise faster than women.
It's biological.

If I let you in
I would be dead now.

Küsse bisse, das reimt sich

She said:
You slice through my heart at the root.
I still must entertain some kind of
mad hope.
Otherwise why am I still here?

NOW I GIVE UP

She said:
The problem is that you always
take the easy way out.
Basically you're a coward.

He said:
Who cares.
I won't take criticism.
In my world I am right
and everyone loves me.

She said:

You are always so dead certain

why other men

diss

betray

exploit

their wives.

Look in the mirror.

She said:

Isn't everything pretence as far as you're concerned:

pretend intimacy

pretend distance

pretend husband

pretend father.

He said:

You misinterpret everything.

You have no

bloody idea

about anything at all.

Old bitch.

Why don't you try and achieve something instead.

She said:
You used to beg for forgiveness
or act like a sad puppy
nuzzle up against me
hands shoved
in trouser pockets
shoulders hunched
wet eyes.

And I always forgave you
we laughed
we carried on
living and loving.

But we always ended up at square one.
It was a mystery.
You'd instantly forget what had
caused our schism.
It could hardly be alluded to.

And that is how I have come to be living
a completely meaningless
inauthentic life.

Mauvaise foi

She said:
Did you thank me for
running with a bedpan and food
all summer
when you said your back had given out
so I couldn't leave you.

She said:
When I bring up the fact
that my female friends
die at seventy
you say it's out of
spite.

Is there no end to your unpleasantness?

She said:
You attacked me

knocked me down in the bathroom
sprained two of my fingers
because you said I provoked you.

Pathetic wanker.

He said:
No-one believes you anyway.

Where did your animosity
towards me come from?

I've always avoided bringing up
genuine differences of opinion
to ensure domestic harmony.

Do we really have to think the same?

She said:
No
but we have to respect
each other.

He said:
I reach for the stars

but you have a healthier relationship
to your work.
It's doled out in nice manageable chunks.
Not too much for you.

She said:
Don't be so insulting.
You hardly know what I do during the day.

He said:
You occupy yourself with a little sect.

She said:
Yes half of everything that exists is female.

He said:
You meant a lot
to me
and still do.

But it's absurd to
want to rule
my life.
You used to think
I was pointless

playing marbles
with the boys.

She said:
You knew I was a feminist
when I picked you up out of the gutter
and gave you a life.

WHEN I'M SIXTY-FOUR

He said:
I thought feminism was uninteresting.
It would drain off you in time.

He said:
A man must decide in his own house.

I believe in nature.
The woman is inferior to the man.
That's the way it's always been.
And how it's going to stay.

No-one listens to you anyway.
You have no status.
You are too stupid.

She said:
We haven't loved each other
for years.

Once we were invincible
because we each viewed ourselves
through each other's infatuated eyes.

Don't you ever miss those days?

She said:
How did we get through
this autumn.
I see the world as greasy.
No sharp colours
just shades of grey.

I have shuffled along
half-heartedly
Don't remember.
There's no point to anything.

What am I doing in this marriage
this civilisation
this family
this world?

OH THE LONELINESS!

She said:

Sometimes my hatred is so strong

it leaches out of me as if I had worms.

There has to be an end to my emotions.

I dream of the day

when I don't feel anything at all.

He said:

You have decided

to get rid of me.

She said:

I long beyond reason

for a man who wishes me well.

He said:

A man who runs

your errands for you

you mean.

IT WOULD BE STRANGE TO FEEL

YOUR HEAVY HEAD AGAINST MY BREAST

She said:

Do you remember a wonderful night
when I got through to you.
You said you understood and that
we had to solve the problems in our life
together.

He said:
Bollocks.
The very next day I realised
you had been being unreasonable as usual.

She said:
But you didn't inform me
of your change of opinion.

I was happy for weeks
before I realised
you had manipulated me
again

One simply becomes poisoned
by your constant double-dealing.

The double entry bookkeeping of slyness.
And then the low
contemptuous
pitiful
blaming everything on me.
It's too much.

We have an *ad hoc* relationship.

TODAY YOU ARE THE PERSON I LIVE WITH

He said:
I am not as single-track
unimaginative as you.
I am a person with capacity.
Can change.

Principles are for moralising
political
dimwits.

She said:
You've made your bed
and I've got to lie in it
you mean.

He said:

Stop harping on all that crap.

He said:
When I was young I was terrified
of social failure.
It almost happened.
You know.

She said:
Then I came and rescued you.
Gave you a home
where you settled down to work
on your career.

I ought to be hung in the square
by my toes.

As a warning to others.

He said:
Life had meaning then.

She said:
Do you remember Matisse's *La conversation*
at the Hermitage.

The symbol of our love:
the man in pyjamas
the woman in her dressing gown
a conversation with paradise
in the background.

He said:
The man is wearing painter's clothes.
He's an artist.
taking a break.

Is it lunch soon
he asks his wife.

She said:
You hate me.

Amor per me non ha per me non ha

He said:

Comradeship.

We're not some gay couple.

She said:

You seemed God-like to me.

Now – demonic.

I SEEM TO MYSELF DEAD

OR VERY NEAR

He said:

You are presumptuous

because you want to

reach my heights.

She said:

What gain they for this trinket

sought throughout the world.

Cold eyes

red face

twisted penis.

She said:

You fling clichés at me:

"life has its ups and downs".
Random moods
"everything's shit"
psychosomatic symptoms
your back hurts
your leg
your heart.

Insult
women's base motives
talk about "negroes".

And then you claim
you're so better educated
than I am.

He said:
Humanity has two options:
fascism or
petty-bourgeois egotism.

Your option
isn't even on the map.

She said:

I can't believe in the happy few.

I've seen you

you who are supposed to be the elite

and I go my own way.

I'd rather

love

think

live.

He said:

Yes yes yes.

In the end you'll probably

get me where you want me –

total demythologisation.

It's hard to bear.

But without you

I would lose

the will to live.

She said:
What you actually hate about me
is that I always took you
at your word.

It counts against me now
because you have come to prefer
people you can dupe
buy
pay off
pull the wool
over the eyes of.

I love the person you no longer want to be.

I can't be bought.
Can't be duped.
I'm a free person.

He said:
I don't like your ideology.

She said:
The person I loved
was a man capable
of being happy
that I was happy.

Who once even
wished me well too
without ulterior motives.

Who could tell me
what he was thinking
unguarded
who sought and received my understanding
who could laugh at
human shortcomings
his own
mine and other people's
with me.

A tender-hearted man.
A man with an inquiring mind

and a sense of humour.
Who enjoyed discussion
and didn't always turn aggressive
if he wasn't proved right.

A man who lit up
when I appeared.
Who burrowed down so close to me
in bed every night.

He did exist.
You have probably forgotten him
but I haven't.

HIS LEFT HAND IS UNDER MY HEAD
AND HIS RIGHT HAND EMBRACES ME

She said:
My beloved used to send postcards from Paris:
"Hello my darling piglet.
As soon as I get an idea
I start to explain it to you
but to empty air.
It must be possible
to live and work together."

That was the man I loved.

He said:
God.
That was exactly what
I was trying to tell you
we can't have.

Not these kinds of tirades.
Never ever.
I refuse to engage
with what you are saying.
I could
but it wouldn't accomplish
anything.

She said
I hate your scheming duplicity.
Doesn't it make you tired?
Always lying to yourself and other people?

I'm not saying it to hurt you.

She said:
Now that it will all soon be over
and you have no more points to score
is it completely impossible
that you could accept
how I experienced
the change in you.

He said:
I don't know what you mean
by accept.
I don't intend to go back to
you incessantly condemning
who I am
and what I stand for.

It's brilliant to be able to enjoy
what one finds amusing
without a bad conscience.

Being allowed to be low-brow
if you want to be low-brow
and high-brow
if you want to be high-brow.

He said:
I don't want
any more finger-wagging
and proposals to reform me
in what life I have left.

She said:
It wasn't an attempt to reform you.
It was love.
I swear.
I loved you
because you weren't like me.

He said:
The expression
"the change in you"

bothers me

for a start.

I don't intend to agree

to dislike myself.

That sort of thing makes you ill.

She said:

Yes ask me.

He said:

Your view of me changed.

That much is true.

Everything else is sniping

and it's better

to ignore that.

I can accept your experience

in the sense

that I know that you have it

and that I don't resent it.

So if that's

what you mean

then yes absolutely
it is possible.

He said:
But in return
you have to get used to the fact
that my experience is different
and is unaffected by yours.

If you could let go of the question of guilt
we would be well on the way
towards a brighter future.

She said:
What do you mean by let go of the question of guilt?
I never lied to you.
I never mocked you.
I never hit you.

You owe me my life.

He said:
Bullshit.
If you've been kicked
and had your ears boxed

a few dozen times
that's overstating it.

I have not abused you.

What are you?
A feminist bitch
out for revenge.

He said:
Don't come back.

She said:
You can't lock me out.
That's appalling.
I can't even take the bike if I haven't got the key.
And where am I going to sleep?

She said:
It is not OK
to throw my laptop
down the stairs.
Don't you get that?

YOU DON'T RAISE A HAND TOWARDS YOUR SISTER

He said:

Forgive my brutality.

But you're a sanctimonious cow

think you're so perfect.

She said:

You have no self-insight.

Your stupidity is carved in stone.

You're a living mummy.

Wake up.

Life is being lived here in our home.

He said:
I have always loved you
wanted to be with you
been happy when I saw you.

When you came home
you lit up the room.
But now you spew out things
that are just fantasies about me.

She said:
No human being has the right
to oppress the one they love.

He said:
No
you are right about that.
I have never considered

I have the right to oppress
or torment you.

If I ever did
it was due to
a misunderstanding
not cruelty.

She said:
I go around
like a graven image in my life
carved in wood
just so as not to risk
feeling hope.

Never-ending excruciating unhappiness
day and night.
It's like coping with sexual trauma –
to survive the abuse
you have to make yourself
dumb
emotionless
transport yourself
somewhere else.

LE RIRE DE LA MÉDUSE

He said:
Stop your revolting poisonous drivel.
You are far and away the most
frightening person
I have ever met.

I was afraid of my mother
but at least she could be distracted
when she was on the warpath.

She said:
You know I'm right
and you hate me for it.

She said:
Love is wishing the other well.
Daring to step beyond your fear
opening up
listening
trying
understanding.

Not deciding
pounding the table with your fist
spouting empty phrases:
The Man must rule over the Woman.

She said:
You just remember
the awful things I said
not your terrifying
words of power.

I have never got through to you.
You're simply unreachable.
You're not human
you're made of Teflon.

He said:
You have all the power in our relationship.

She said:
My love has run out
nothing left.

No-one can go on without a modicum of support.

Every time we talk seriously
you defend your position
hurl abuse at me.
My unhappiness
the life you have regulated in detail
is my own fault
so you have to rule over me
beat me down
and I just have to like it.

He said:
You are my bridle.

She said:
No
Your pride is your bridle.

She said:
What did I think I saw in you?
A certain winning
helplessness at life
that made me
fool that I was
think you were seeking your equal
and soulmate in me.

It was more that you were looking for
a gorgeous arse
full-board
all inclusive
replication of your genes.

Now:
a set of stale prejudices
false wisdom
prettily packaged style.

And I fell for it.

TEACH ME TO ROT LIKE A SINGLE LEAF

He said:
So a man isn't
allowed to be a man
any longer?

She said:
I was your marketing ace
until you found a better stage
in the seat of power.
You must see

that I feel
dumped.

She said:
Lifelong bonds
are the most important thing
between people
you said at the dinner.
They mustn't be broken.

But what if only one of you is
nurturing the bond?

He said:
You are impossible.
Give me a chance.

She said:
When you say give me a chance
I know you're thinking
how you're going to manipulate me
more cleverly next time.

He said:
Piffle.

She said:

The only stimulus you react to

is instant admiration.

The Board is your fix.

If losing me

doesn't help

nothing will.

He said:

With mother it was important

to stay the course.

Never answer.

She always gave up in the end.

He said:
What you are saying now
means you made a mistake
that time we
sat in the café by the harbour.

You should have answered when I asked
whether we should divorce
immediately.

I was prepared for the news
and would have taken it calmly
however sad it may have been.

Now it is considerably more difficult
because I no longer
think we would be right
to go our separate ways.

Of course the train-wreck
has to do with
our discord and unhappiness.

We have to sort out
our mutual relationship.

She said:
I don't know.
It's as if there's a thick filter between
my old feelings for you
and the way it feels
since the latest outbursts.

Why this outstretched hand now?
You can see distrust has gained a foothold.

There's so much about you
I can't stand any more.

He said:
My darling.
If you look sensibly
at the situation that has arisen
it is fairly clear

that the best solution
would be for us to divorce
as soon as possible
and start to live
our separate lives.

But things like this
aren't decided
on common sense
but on feelings.

What feelings
you ask.
The feelings that return
when we think about how
things used to be
once upon a time.

I've been thinking
and reached conclusions
sometimes one way
sometimes the other.

But what finally
convinced me

that it would be wrong of us to give up
is the memory of what it felt like
when we reconciled
in the café by the harbour.

To me it was completely unexpected.
I went to our meeting
with a sense of
going to my own execution.

I was certain that
you were about to draw up
terms for divorce.

When that didn't happen
I was overwhelmed by a sense of happiness
that I can't recall feeling
since our first years together.

I saw you and from that day on
I see nothing in the world but you.

It was as if the whole world
was transformed.
Like when a picture turns

from black and white into colour.
No.
More than that.

Suddenly we were talking to each other
like close friends.

Everything was fun
like it used to be.

And that feeling didn't end
when we cycled home.
It stayed with me.

He said:
You can say that I then
destroyed it
with my outbursts
but the issue
is a little more complicated
than that.

What does all this tell me?
It tells me simply
that in our innermost hearts

we still
want each other.

Against all reason.

But I am convinced
that both you and I
would rejoice inside
once more
however many times more
if the slightest opportunity presented itself
to be truly reconciled and
start a new life together.

She said:
That's true.
I too was overcome by hope
against all the odds.

It was the first time
in our life together
that you had asked me
what you could do
to make me a little happier.
I was stunned by happiness.

Suddenly my beloved sat before me.
The world regained its scent and flavour
my body its contours.

Sensuality rose like sap in spring.
It was worth living.

Then Mr Hyde emerged again.
It took six days.

THE KNIFE-THROWER'S WOMAN

He said:
You must take what I said
at face value.

Why this outstretched hand now?
Because if we don't
reach out to each other now
it will be forever too late.

I can't go through
any more trials by ordeal in the form of
your rejection
for weeks or months.

I'm asking you to think very carefully.

He said:
It has nothing
to do
with my social façade.
In the current crisis
that is beside the point.

She said:
When the crisis is over
your social façade
will take over again.

I know you.
Your protestations of love
are short-lived.

He said:
If I don't want to delve into
the causes of my most recent outbursts
at this precise moment
it's because I don't want to
put the blame on someone else.

Perhaps I've learned something.

He said:
I have to know
whether I am to
forget you or not.

Whether I am to rearrange my life
on the assumption
that you are part of it
or on the assumption
that you are not.

I don't think it's too late to ask the question.

She said:
I'm afraid of you.
Your brutality
your self-love
your arrogance.

It won't go away.

He said:
Unsympathetic characteristics are not

in themselves
an obstacle to love.

I don't like you but I love you
as the old hit
went.

YOU'VE REALLY GOT A HOLD ON ME

That's how it is.
It's all about what one wants.

She said:
What an offensive proposal.
And you don't even know why.

He said:
What were you thinking
when we sat in that café?

Who was I to you then?
It seems baffling.

She said:
Had you said that
ten years
six years
three years
one year ago
I might have been brave enough.

But then you were mute.
Deaf
Scornful

Manipulative
Rude
Raging.

I was on my knees
praying for my life.

He said:
The heart is so odd
that when I heard you
speak in that tone of voice
I hadn't heard for years
deep inside me
I became completely calm.

The expression gentle as a lamb
would for once
not have been out of place.

At that moment
you could have asked me
practically anything.

I would have been delighted
to hurl myself into the water

and fetch you a dandelion
from the other side of the bay.

That moment was worth
long periods in hell.

After it I was buoyed up
by incredible optimism for the future
as I think
you were
too.

She said:
Keep your dandelions.
Hit me less.
Love me more.

He said:
What subsequently transpired
was just as unexpected
to me as it was to you.

I felt you were
somewhere else
because you were

about to go away.

Yes
then it all boiled over
as they say.

In my suspicious mind
you were preoccupied with
what you were going to say
at various conferences
in the week ahead.
You were already
halfway out of the door.

I realise
that was all
completely unfair.

It does not excuse
my loss of control
in what followed.

I truly regret
behaviour that frightened you.

He said:
What has probably happened
is that in recent years
my natural quick temper
has grown stronger
roughly the same time as I developed
raised blood pressure
and back problems
from my work.

I don't know what one can do about
disproportionate anger
in purely medical terms.

One doesn't want to take
sedatives and turn into
a drugged-out care home case
with slow movements
and slurred speech.

My beta-blockers
help with everyday irritations
but they are powerless
against the subterranean undercurrents.

I don't feel at ease
in my life
any more.

I realise you may
find this boring
and deeply uninteresting.

She said:
Violence can be a symptom of
creeping frontal lobe dementia.

It changes people's personalities.

If you were diagnosed
with something like that
I wouldn't leave you in the lurch.

You are
were
the man in my life.

She said:
But I fear for my safety
when I'm near you.

If you raise a hand
to take a glass out of the cupboard
I duck.

I don't stand in corners any more.
Preferably in the doorway
or within sight of the exit.

Panic attacks are my most faithful friend.

He said:
It torments me
terribly
that we can't talk to each other
like human beings.

I try to think
about what happened
as little as possible.

With minimal success
it is true but still.

I go to bed early
to make the days slightly shorter.

I try to repress
the immense sadness
I feel.

Because if I felt it
it would crush me.

She said:
Your gallows conversion
is tragic.

I shed a tear
but I can't quite manage
to believe you.

He said:
The rights and wrongs in this matter
would currently appear to be
a first-world problem.

If only it was quiet
perhaps you might realise
I mean you no harm.
I'm not hoping
for anything at all.

Not even for you to understand
and respect me.

But I still have to try.
I appeal for a truce.

She said:
I don't want anything either.
If I could only risk believing
your regret is sincere.

He said:
The question of guilt is of no interest.
Women will keep going on about it.

One must allow
different to be equal.

She said:
Different was not equal
in our marriage.

He said:
One has to be able to draw a line
and move on.

She said:
Not without *Wiedergutmachung.*

There is mercy for everyone.
I will forgive you
with pleasure
with all of my heart.

Und ewig wäre sie dann mein

All you have to do
is ask my forgiveness.

If you can't do that
you don't understand
what you did to the woman you loved.
And will repeat it.

ALL DAYS ALL NIGHTS

He said:
I don't have to do anything.

She said:
Let love be the gravestone lying on my life.

He said:

I know what you women are like.

You're all snowflakes.

She said:

Welcome home

I say

to myself.

Appendix

DANCE OF DEATH August Strindberg, Dödsdansen
(Dance of Death) (1900)

A *kiss, a bite, The two should rhyme, for one who truly loves, with
all her heart, can easily mistake them.* Heinrich von Kleist,
Penthesilea (1808), translation by Joel Agee, Michael di
Capua Books 1998

argumentum ex silentio – argument from silence, conclusion
based on a lack of evidence

You said I killed you – haunt me, then! Emily Brontë, Wuthering
Heights (1847)

Brudertier, Du – You brother animal. Lou Andreas-Salomé
in a letter to her lover, the psychoanalyst Viktor Tausk
(1913)

Gaslight. Thriller by George Cukor starring Ingrid Bergman
and Charles Boyer (1944)

Après nous le déluge – After us the Flood. Attributed to Mad-
ame de Pompadour (1721–1764), lover of Louis XV

*Jedes Leben sei zu führen, Wenn man sich nicht selbst vermißt; Alles
könne man verlieren, Wenn man bleibe, was man ist.* There's
not a life we need refuse, If our true self we do not miss,
There's not a thing one may not lose, If one remains the
man he is. Johann Wolfgang von Goethe, West-Eastern
Divan (1819) VIII Book of Zuleika, Xxi Zuleika. Translated by Edward Dowden, (1914)

Golden lads and girls all must, As chimney-sweepers, come to dust.
William Shakespeare, Cymbeline

All Rome trembled before him! E avanti a lui tremava tutta
   Roma! Tosca's response after having stabbed Scarpia,
   the chief of police who attempted to rape her in Puccini's
   opera Tosca (1900)

You can get a lot done between the tears. Man kan hinna mycket
   mellan tårarna Elin Wägner, Pennskaftet (1910)

The Night of the Tribades, Tribadernas natt Play by P O Enquist
   (1975)

Was nun kleiner Mann Little man, what now? Hans Fallada's novel
   Kleiner Mann – was nun? (1932)

RELY ON A MAN AND YOU DESERVE SLAPPING
   Lita på en karl man skulle ha stryk, Moa Martinson,
   Kyrkbröllop (1938)

WILFUL DISREGARD Novel by Lena Andersson (2013)
   translated by Sarah Death (Picador 2015).

Deus ex machina Literally God from a machine. Stage solution
   from ancient theatre in which a God was sent down to
   rescue a character from a dangerous situation

Wagner's Senta and Elsa – Senta in the Flying Dutchman,
   who saves the hero by dying for him. Elsa in Lohengrin
   who breaks her promise to her husband by forcing him
   to reveal his identity.

Le repos du guerrier Warrior's rest Novel by Christiane Rochefort
   (1958) translated by Lowell Bair 1959

Forførarens dagbog The Seducer's Diary by Søren Kierkegaard
   (1843)

dürstend nach Ruhm und Ehre – Thirsting for reputation and
   honour

Lasciatemi morire – Let me die. Ariadne's lament on the island of Naxos following her abandonment by Theseus, Claudio Monteverdi's lost opera L'Arianna (1608)

Of terror was the mail-coat cast and of shame Men av skräck var brynjan gjuten/ och av skam Karin Boye, Härdarna (1927) translated by David McDuff, Hearths, Karin Boye The Complete Poems.

Il capo di capo Should be Il capo dei capi, the top boss in the Italian Mafia.

HUGO RASK WAS NOT UNDER ANY OBLIGATION TO LOVE HER HUGO RASK VAR INTE SKYLDIG ATT ÄLSKA HENNE Lena Andersson, Wilful Disregard (2013/2015) translated by Sarah Death.

Mimetic desire, René Girard, Mensonge romantique et vérité romanesque (1961) Deceit, Desire and the Novel translated by Yvonne Freccero (1966)

WHAT'S IN A NAME IT IS NOR HAND NOR FOOT NOR ANY OTHER PART BELONGING TO A MAN William Shakespeare, Romeo and Juliet (1597)

Cold heart beneath the glitter/Grey skin, bright ribbon curled. Anna Maria Lenngren, Pojkarne (The Boys) (1797). The last verse of the poem reads:

Hvad ger då denna Tärnan,
Så sökt I alla land?
Kallt hjerta under stjernan,
Gul hy och granna band.

What gain they for this trinket
So sought throughout the world
cold heart beneath the glitter
grey skin, bright ribbon curled

Aus den Augen aus dem Sinn Out of sight, out of mind

He's the sort of man who says what he thinks and then
believes it – "Sådan är han; han säger vad han tycker,
och så tror han på det." August Strindberg, Dödsdansen
(1900)

HURRY MY DEAREST COME HURRY TO LOVE ME
/ MINUTE BY MINUTE THE DAYS THEY GROW
DARK. SKYNDA ATT ÄLSKA DAGARNA MÖRK-
NAR MINUT FÖR MINUT Tove Jansson, "Höstvisa"
Autumn song (1965)

Come in I'll give you shelter from the storm Bob Dylan,
Blood on the Tracks (1975)

Advertise or go under, Dorothy L. Sayers, Murder Must
Advertise (1933)

GIVE ME A GRAVE IN THE LAND OF MY BIRTH
GIV MIG EN GRAV PÅ FOSTERJORD, Zacharias
Topelius, Julvisa (1887)

BE WHITE MAN'S SLAVE VARA VIT MANS SLAV
Sonja Åkesson Äktenskapsfrågan (The Marriage Question) in Husfrid (1963)

Now I have dreamt two nights in a row that I was happy
and carried a knife in my hand, a bloody knife, and my
heart was as light as a bird. Dreams mean nothing, but I
wonder if I shall see the same dream one more time. Nu
har jag drömt etc. Edith Södergran, »Undret«, Landet
som icke är (1925). Complete poems Edith Södergran
translated David McDuff Bloodaxe Books 1984.

Alone I came, alone I must go. My free heart has no brother.
Ensam har jag kommit etc Edith Södergran, Ensam,
Framtidens skugga (1920) Complete poems Edith Söder-
gran translated David McDuff Bloodaxe Books 1984.

Dovre witch Character in Selma Lagerlöf's Gösta Berlings
Saga (1891) (The Saga of Gösta Berling)

Besserwisser Know-it-all

Negging the use of backhanded compliments by pick-up
    artists. The Swedish reference is to Neggraggare in Liv
    Strömqvist's graphic novel, Prins Charles känsla (The
    Prince Charles Feeling) (2010)

Every sperm is sacred Monthy Python, The Meaning of Life
    (1983)

OH WOMEN OF THE PAST – O FORNA TIDERS
    KVINNOR Selma Lagerlöf, Gösta Berlings saga (The
    Saga of Gösta Berling) (1891)

SOMETHING IN THE WAY SHE MOVES George Har-
    rison, Something, The Beatles, Abbey Road (1969)

SHE HAD BEEN ALLOWED TO BE NEAR HIM AS
    LONG AS SHE DID NOT SEE HIM FOR WHAT
    HE WAS. HON FICK VARA I HANS NÄRHET SÅ
    LÄNGE HON INTE SÅG VEM HAN VAR Lena
    Andersson, Egenmäktigt förfarande (2013) Sarah Death
    Wilful Disregard (2015)

Professor von X Virginia Woolf, A Room of One's Own
    (1929)

L'amour est enfant de bohème, Love is a gypsy's child, George
    Bizet's opera Carmen (1875)

Strong people don't bend/They break and snap Märta
    Tikkanen, Århundradets kärlekssaga (1978) (Love Story
    of the Century)

SET ME AS A SEAL UPON YOUR HEART. Bible Song
    of Songs Chapter 8, verse 6

DIDI AND GOGO Samuel Beckett Waiting for Godot
    (1952)

THE TAMING OF THE SHREW William Shakespeare
(1590)

*I want to be dealing with simple sensible people, not this smarmy herd
of idiots.* Jag vill ha med enkelt vettigt folk att göra och
inte med denna sliskiga hjord av fjantar Moa Martinson
in a letter to Karl Olsson at the publishers Tiden 13 July
1938

WHEN YOU WALK THROUGH A STORM hold your
head up high and don't be afraid of the dark. You'll never walk alone. Carousel, Rogers and Hammerstein

THE MOOR HAS DONE HIS WORK. THE MOOR
MAY GO Friedrich Schiller, Fiesco or Fiesco's Conspir-
acy at Genoa (1782)

War alles umsonst Was it all for nothing, Christa Wolf, City of
Angels or The overcoat of Dr Freud (2010)

A MAN MUST CARRY THE MOTHER OF HIS CHIL-
DREN IN HIS HANDS EN MAN SKA BÄRA SINA
BARNS MOR PÅ SINA HÄNDER Agneta Pleijel, En
vinter i Stockholm (A Winter in Stockholm) (1997)

Küsse, bisse, das reimt sich A kiss, a bite/the two should rhyme,
Heinrich von Kleist, Penthesilea (1808)

Mauvaise foi The fundamental concept of "bad faith" in ex-
istentialism used by Simone de Beauvoir in The Second
Sex (1949) about a woman who gives up her identity out
of love for a man

Half of everything that exists is female *Ja, hälften av alla som
finns är kvinns,* Wava Stürmer, Vi är många (1973), (We
are many) Women's song book

WHEN I'M SIXTY-FOUR Paul McCartney, The Beatles
Sgt. Pepper's Lonely Hearts Club's Band (1967)

OH THE LONELINESS! Å ENSAMHETEN I DETTA
Karl Ove Knausgård, Cyklopernas land (The Land of
the Cyclopses), Dagens Nyheter 19.5.2015

IT WOULD BE STRANGE TO FEEL YOUR HEAVY
HEAD AGAINST MY BREAST. DET VORE UN-
DERLIGT ATT KÄNNA DITT TUNGA HUVUD
MOT MITT BRÖST "Det vore underligt att känna,
en enda natt, en natt som denna, ditt tunga huvud mot
mitt bröst" Edith Södergran, "Dagen svalnar...", Dikter
(1916). Translated by David McDuff, Complete Poems

TODAY YOU ARE THE PERSON I LIVE WITH.
IDAG ÄR DU DEN JAG BOR MED Märta Tikkanen,
Århundradets kärlekssaga (Love Story of the Century)
(1978)

Amor per me non ha per me non ha She loves me, she loves me
not, King Philip of Spain's aria in Guiseppe Verdi's
opera Don Carlos (1867)

I SEEM TO MYSELF DEAD OR VERY NEAR Sappho
(c. 630–570 BC), fragment 31, translation by Vivie
Humphreys

HIS LEFT HAND IS UNDER MY HEAD AND HIS
RIGHT HAND EMBRACES ME Song of Songs
Chapter 8 verse 3

YOU DON'T RAISE A HAND TOWARDS YOUR
SISTER. MAN BÄR INT HAND PÅ SYSTRO SIN
Peter Sandström, Syster, Till dig som saknas (2012)

Le Rire de la Méduse 1975 (the laugh of the medusa), Hélène
Cixous translated into English by Keith and Paula
Cohen (1976)

Teach me to rot like a single leaf LÄR MIG ATT RUTTNA
SOM ETT ENKELT BLAD Ann Jäderlund, Som en
gång varit äng (1988)

I saw you and from that day on I see nothing in the world
   but you .Jag såg dig och från denna dag jag endast dig i
   världen ser, Johan Henric Kellgren, "Den nya Skapelsen
   eller Inbildningens Verld" (1790) "The New Creation, or
   the World of the Imagination"

THE KNIFE-THROWER'S WOMAN KNIVKASTA-
   RENS KVINNA Kerstin Ekman (1990)

YOU'VE REALLY GOT A HOLD ON ME Smokey
   Robinson, The Miracles (1962)

Wiedergutmachung Reparations, repairing the evil one has
   done. Term used for the compensation Germany decided
   to pay to the victims of the Nazis in 1953.

Und ewig wäre sie dann mein And then she would be mine
   forever, Tamino's love aria Dies Bildnis ist bezaubernd
   schön, Wolfgang Amadeus Mozart's opera, The Magic
   Flute (1791)

ALL DAYS ALL NIGHTS ALLA DAGAR ALLA NÄT-
   TER, play by Margareta Garpe (1992)

Let love be the gravestone lying on my life Anna Akhmatova
   (1914), Confusion, in Rosary, the Complete Poems of
   Anna Akhmatova p. 133 ed Roberta Reeder, translated
   by Judith Hemschemeyer,(1914)